Spotlight on the 13 Colonies
Birth of a Nation

★ ★ ★ ★ ★ ★ ★ ★ ★ ★ ★ ★

THE COLONY OF
VIRGINIA

Jackie Heckt

PowerKiDS
press™

NEW YORK

Published in 2016 by The Rosen Publishing Group, Inc.
29 East 21st Street, New York, NY 10010

Editor: Caitie McAneney
Book Design: Andrea Davison-Bartolotta

Library of Congress Cataloging-in-Publication Data

Heckt, Jackie.
The colony of Virginia / by Jackie Heckt.
p. cm. — (Spotlight on the 13 colonies: Birth of a nation)
Includes index.
ISBN 978-1-4994-0587-3 (pbk.)
ISBN 978-1-4994-0588-0 (6 pack)
ISBN 978-1-4994-0591-0 (library binding)
1. Virginia — History — Colonial period, ca. 1600 - 1775 — Juvenile literature. 2. Virginia — History — 1775 - 1865 — Juvenile literature. I. Title.
F229.H43 2016
975.5/02—d23

Manufactured in the United States of America

CPSIA Compliance Information: Batch #WS15PK: For further information contact Rosen Publishing, New York, New York at 1-800-237-9932.

Contents

Expanding the Empire

Queen Elizabeth I had big plans for England during her rule in the late 1500s. She wanted to make England a strong empire by expanding its trade. Like many European kingdoms, England began exploring the world for new resources. The Americas, which became known as the New World, were believed to be full of opportunity and riches. Elizabeth granted patents to people willing to settle land under England's name. One such patent was given to well-known adventurer Sir Walter Raleigh.

In 1584, Philip Amadas and Arthur Barlowe commanded two ships to North America's eastern coast under orders from Raleigh. They explored the East Coast and mapped the land, claiming it for England. Raleigh named the land Virginia, although it was much bigger than the state of Virginia today. At the time, there were no other Europeans there. However, the area was home to many groups of Native Americans. While the English encountered native tribes, they wouldn't accept help or **hospitality** from them.

Pasquenoke

Sir Walter Raleigh

This map shows English ships arriving in Virginia. To the left, you can see the island of Roanoke, which is where Sir Walter Raleigh attempted to build the first English settlement.

Trinety harbor

Lost Roanoke

With Virginia claimed, Raleigh worked to establish a colony on Roanoke Island, which is now part of North Carolina. In 1585, Raleigh sent 108 men to settle the area. These settlers met the Roanoke Indians, a group of natives who spoke an Algonquian language and lived along the East Coast. Problems between the settlers and the Roanoakes caused the settlers to abandon the land in 1586.

In 1587, Raleigh sent another group of settlers to Roanoke, but they all mysteriously disappeared by 1590. All they left behind was the word "Croatoan" carved into a post and "Cro" carved into a tree. The colony on Roanoke Island became known as the Lost Colony.

In 1603, James I became king of England. James I took away Raleigh's **charter** and gave it to the Virginia Company, which was a group of **investors** from London. Soon after obtaining the charter, the Virginia Company sent more people to Virginia to settle and make money for Great Britain.

On August 18, 1587, Virginia Dare was born. She was the first English child born in North America. She disappeared with the rest of the Lost Colony, but there are legends about what may have happened to her.

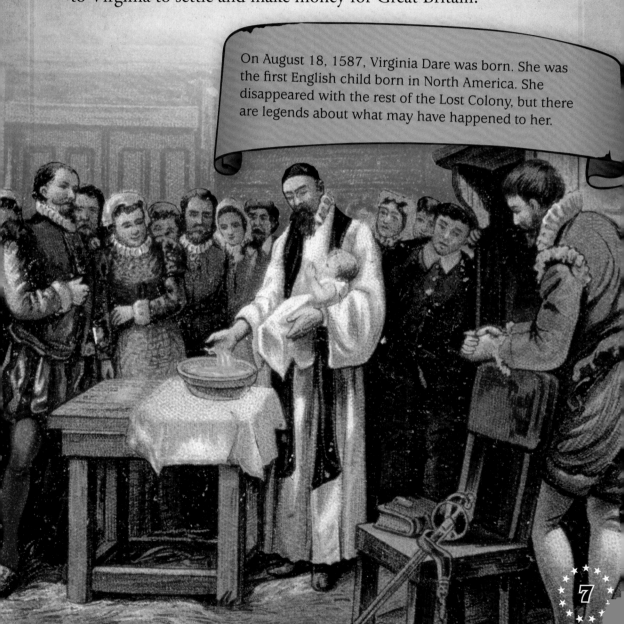

A Colony at Jamestown

The Virginia Company sent more settlers from England, who landed in Virginia on May 14, 1607. They settled along a river they named the James River and called their settlement Jamestown. This was the first English settlement in North America to survive the early stages of settlement.

The settlers met another Algonquian-speaking tribe that lived nearby, whom the settlers called the Powhatans. This tribe helped the English survive their first few winters, but when food was low or the English took Indian territory, fighting would start. The settlers built a wooden fence around their settlement to protect themselves.

The real danger for the settlers, however, was the swamp near the settlement. The swamp had salt water, and when the settlers drank it, they became very sick. The swamp also attracted mosquitoes, which carried illnesses such as **malaria**. Some settlers died from these illnesses, while others became unable to work. There were 104 original settlers in the Jamestown colony, and after just a year, only 38 were left.

In the beginning, the Powhatan tribe was suspicious of the English, but thought trading between them might benefit both sides. When they got along, the Powhatans could give food to the English in exchange for metal tools, glass beads, and guns.

Struggling to Survive

The Virginia Colony faced many challenges in its early days and saw many illnesses and deaths. The colonists had agreed to work for the Virginia Company, mining for gold, but many times it was hard just to stay alive.

Captain John Smith became president of the Jamestown government in 1608. He worked hard to get the colonists to succeed, making the rule, "He who does not work, will not eat." Under his leadership, Jamestown flourished. However, Smith had to leave Jamestown in 1609 due to a gunpowder accident.

The winter after Smith left was known as the Starving Time. Colonists and supplies were sent from England to Jamestown, but never made it. The boat sank near Bermuda.

Pocahontas

Without Smith's leadership or new supplies, food became so scarce that many colonists starved to death. Crime and illness spread, and there were even reports of cannibalism. Of 214 settlers at Jamestown, only 60 survived the Starving Time.

In 1607, John Smith was captured by the natives and brought to Chief Powhatan. Legend has it that as Smith was on trial to be put to death, Powhatan's young daughter Pocahontas persuaded her father to let Smith go.

The Plant That Saved Virginia

During the Starving Time, it seemed as if the Jamestown settlement would fail. However, the next spring, a boat came with supplies, and more settlers were sent to the colony.

The Virginia Company wanted the settlers to work harder and increase the profits of the colony. In 1618, the company **introduced** a system of granting land to colonists and new settlers, called the headright system. John Rolfe, an English farmer and colonist, encouraged settlers to farm tobacco.

Starving Time

Rolfe believed tobacco would be a good **cash crop** because it was becoming popular to smoke tobacco in Europe. Tobacco became the first big American industry. In 1618, colonists sent nearly 40,000 pounds (18,160 kg) of tobacco back to England.

While the population of Virginia rose, the debt of the Virginia Company also rose. No gold was found, and tobacco was introduced too late. In 1624, the Virginia Company lost its charter. King James I took control, making Virginia the first royal colony in North America.

Settlers grew their tobacco on large farms called plantations. Then, the tobacco was harvested and sent to England in barrels.

13

Slavery Comes to Virginia

As plantations grew in Virginia, it became clear that settlers would need more help in the fields. In 1619, a Dutch ship arrived with around 20 Africans. They were put to work on plantations, probably as **indentured servants** at first, then later as slaves. The use of slaves in Virginia grew slowly at first, but by 1680, the number grew to 3,000 slaves. By 1700, that number grew to over 10,000. It became cheaper to buy a slave than to buy several years of labor from an indentured servant.

The life of a slave was often one of backbreaking work, no pay, and cruel mistreatment. Men, women, and children were stolen from their homes in Africa and sent to America in dirty ships. The ships were so crowded that slaves could barely move. About one in five slaves died on the journey. Once in Virginia, slaves were treated as animals rather than people. If they didn't obey, they were given painful punishments, such as whipping or even death.

newly arrived slaves in Virginia

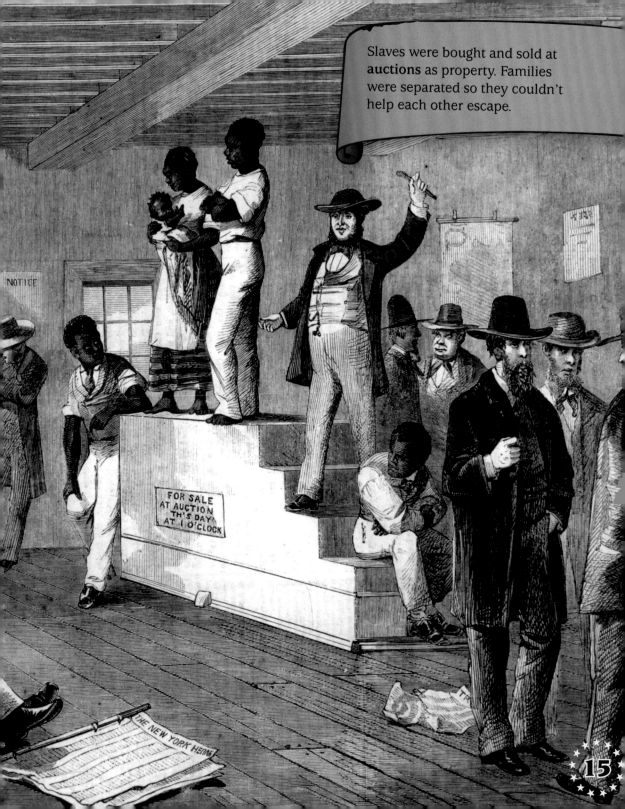

Slaves were bought and sold at **auctions** as property. Families were separated so they couldn't help each other escape.

15

Unrest in the Colonies

In the 1600s and early 1700s, England continued to grow its territory along the eastern coast of North America and establish more colonies. They also fought the French and Indian War. Beginning in 1754, this war was the result of territorial disagreements between France and Great Britain.

By the time the war ended in 1763, England's King George III and **Parliament** decided to tighten their control over the colonies. Taxes were raised to help pay for the war and to pay for soldiers to keep peace between Indians and settlers on the western frontier. The colonists were especially angered over the Stamp Act, which put a tax on all paper goods.

The colonists thought it was unfair to pay taxes passed by leaders an ocean away, for whom they hadn't even voted. The colonists believed in the lawmaking and taxing power of their local assemblies, such as the Virginia House of Burgesses. Established in 1619, this was the first elected **legislature** in the American colonies.

In 1765, Patrick Henry addressed the Virginia House of Burgesses. In his speech, he openly opposed the Stamp Act and said, "If this be treason, make the most of it." His speech was one of the sparks that led to the American Revolution.

Declaring Independence

The colonies banded together to discuss what could be done about their problems with England. The First Continental Congress met in Philadelphia, Pennsylvania, in the autumn of 1774. It gathered together 56 representatives from the colonies. Patrick Henry and George Washington were among those who represented Virginia. The Continental Congress declared that if the unfair British taxes weren't **repealed**, colonists would **boycott** British goods. They wrote a **petition** to King George that stated their complaints.

The American Revolution started in 1775 with the Battles of Lexington and Concord. The Continental Congress met again in 1775 to prepare for war while it continued to work for peace. King George rejected their peace efforts, and a group—including Virginia's Thomas Jefferson—was appointed to write the Declaration of Independence. This document stated that the American colonies had the right to break free from Britain and start their own independent nation. On July 4, 1776, Congress approved the Declaration of Independence, and America was born.

On May 15, 1776, the Virginia Convention voted to instruct the colony's representatives in the Continental Congress to introduce a motion for independence.

A Victory at Yorktown

The colonies may have declared themselves free, but they had to win the war. Americans faced many losses to British troops and suffered many **casualties**. Fortunately, the French joined them in their fight against the British, giving them a chance to win.

The final battle of the American Revolution happened in Virginia at Yorktown. In August 1781, British general Charles Cornwallis led his troops to Yorktown to await much-needed supplies and aid. However, General George Washington led American and French troops to Yorktown. They surrounded the British army and formed a blockade, which stopped British ships from entering the harbor to help.

For three weeks, American and French troops led a **siege** against British troops, firing cannons and guns on Yorktown. Cornwallis finally knew the fight to be hopeless. He surrendered on behalf of the British troops on October 19, 1781. Nearly two years later, Great Britain and the United States signed the Treaty of Paris, a peace settlement between the two countries.

surrender of
General Cornwallis

The Treaty of Paris was signed in Paris, France, on September 3, 1783. As part of the treaty, Great Britain had to recognize the United States as an independent nation.

21

Virginia the State

In 1777, the Continental Congress adopted the Articles of Confederation. It was a set of laws for the new United States of America. However, people were afraid of strong federal government after being mistreated by England's government. Therefore, the laws of the Articles of Confederation were very loose and gave most power to states.

After 10 years, it became clear the United States needed a stronger **constitution**. In May 1787, states sent representatives to Philadelphia to improve the Articles. Instead, they wound up writing a new constitution, and the meetings became known as the Constitutional Convention. Virginia representative James Madison created a plan for the Constitution. Two years later, he also created a set of amendments—or articles—to the Constitution known as the Bill of Rights.

Constitutional Convention representatives signed the Constitution on September 17, 1787. Virginia adopted the Constitution on June 25, 1788. The land where the settlers first landed, where plantations abounded, and where the American Revolution found victory finally became a state.

Glossary

auction: A sale of property at which buyers bid against each other for individual items.

boycott: To join with others in refusing to buy from or deal with a person, nation, or business.

cash crop: An agricultural product grown primarily to sell.

casualty: Someone who is hurt or killed in an accident or a war.

charter: An official agreement from a ruler giving someone permission to do something.

constitution: The basic rules by which a country or state is governed.

hospitality: The friendly treatment of guests.

indentured servant: A person who works for another person for a fixed amount of time as payment of travel or living costs.

introduce: To bring into practice or use.

investor: Someone who gives money for something they hope will bring them more money later.

legislature: A body of people having the power to make laws.

malaria: A disease involving a high fever that's passed from one person to another by mosquito bites.

Parliament: The governmental group in England that makes the country's laws.

petition: A formal way to ask for something to be done.

repeal: To do away with.

siege: A constant attack.

Index

Primary Source List

p. 4–5 *The Arrival of the Englishemen in Virginia.* Created by Theodor de Bry. Colored engraving. Included in *A Brief and True Report of the New Found Land of Virginia* by Thomas Hariot, published in London, England, in 1590.

p. 5 (inset) *Portrait of Sir Walter Raleigh (1522 – 1618), Soldier and Historian.* Created by William Segar. Oil on canvas. 1598. Now kept at the National Gallery of Ireland, Dublin, Ireland.

Websites

Due to the changing nature of Internet links, PowerKids Press has developed an online list of websites related to the subject of this book. This site is updated regularly. Please use this link to access the list: www.powerkidslinks.com/s13c/vir